Sponsors introduction

The concerns of most charities barely featured in the May 1997 election campaign. They were driven off the agenda by tax, the NHS, education and Europe. One hundred days later many charities were stunned by the way in which the new government is openly consulting them, asking them to describe the situations they are trying to tackle and where they think the solutions lie. Some charities are now questioning their future role and how they can maintain their independence from government.

We at BDO Stoy Hayward's Charity Unit are particularly pleased to support the publication of *What Are Charities For?*, coming as it does at a time when the change of government, combined with static levels of personal giving, an increasingly competitive fundraising marketplace, and the impact of a more business-like approach to voluntary sector management are making many of our charity clients question how they can continue to make the best use of their limited resources or even whether they should carry out a fundamental review of how they can best contribute to society.

Our Charity Unit prides itself on taking a holistic approach to its work. When advising our clients we take the wider social, political and economic context in which not-for-profit organisations are operating into account, as well as paying attention to the values and culture of the voluntary sector. This important publication also adopts both a strategic and a practical approach. It helps charity managers and trustees answer the fundamental question 'what are we here for?' and describes practical tools they can use to measure their performance. It suggests new roles they could assume to help them increase their impact on society.

The increasing interest in ethical consumerism and ethical investment is a testament to the fact that, despite the decline in religious belief in society as a whole, many people are looking for a spiritual dimension to their lives, or at least searching for a code of values to live by. New Labour, New Government, New Charities - Joe Saxton suggests that charities seize the moment and become moral leaders, speaking out loudly when they see things that are wrong in our society. Charities should become setters of standards higher than those proscribed by existing laws or government policies; standards which capture the public imagination in a way that makes people voluntarily adhere to them. Charities must also be creators and spreaders of new ideas or approaches to tackling problems. The voluntary sector can take pride in its past achievements. Macmillan Cancer Relief has transformed the way in which health professionals view the needs of people with cancer, Friends of the Earth and Greenpeace put environmental issues on the political agenda, and poor people in the Third World can thank overseas development charities like Oxfam and Christian Aid for helping them through their lobbying work on Third World debt relief.

BDO Stoy Hayward's core business is providing expert advice to growing businesses, both in the for-profit and the not-for-profit sectors. We view change as the catalyst for success. We are proud to be associated with a publication that could change the very fabric of our society.

Kate Kirkland
Director of the Charity Unit
BDO Stoy Hayward

Contents

Part One

Discusses how charities can revisit and redefine both their purpose and their vision to help them to decide what makes them special and to answer the question 'what are we here for?'

Outlines strategies for service provision and creating a coherent portfolio of services with a view to answering the question 'what can we do best?'. It is only by understanding the nature of non-profit service provision that charities can begin to be more effective.

Provides some simple analytical tools to help organisations understand and analyse the services they provide.

Looks at performance measurement in charities and discusses the difficulties of measuring success or progress.

Suggests three roles for charities to help them increase their impact.

Part Two

Twelve charity case studies, based on interviews with charity chief executives, about how charities tackle the issues of purpose and service provision.

A structure for an away-day for senior staff or trustees
Suggestions for performance indicators.

1. Introduction

It takes a rough sea to make a great captain – Anonymous

'What are charities for?' is one of the oldest most frequently asked questions about the voluntary sector. Everyone holds a different idea in their head of what charities should and shouldn't do, and occasionally the media articulates some of these views. Some people are concerned that charities are providing services that really should be provided by the government or that public donations are going to causes that clearly do not deserve them.

But beneath the banner headlines there lie more serious concerns for charities which need to ask themselves how they can make sure their organisation is doing the most it can with its limited resources and how they know if they are being as effective as it is possible to be. More fundamentally they need to ask 'what are we here for?'. The reality is that most charities are not doing everything they want to do, let alone all that their mandates empower them to do. So if an organisation isn't doing everything it could, how does it decide what to do?

For commercial organisations the answer to this question is easy. Making a profit is both the purpose of the organisation and the measure of its effectiveness. Put crudely, more profit this year than last, means a company is doing better this year than it did last year. What's more, competitive selection weeds out sick or weak companies as poor performance is not tolerated for long. And companies enjoy much greater freedom: take-overs, mergers, borrowing, lending, and geographical expansion are all ways in which the good flourish and the poor disappear.

Life is less simple in the voluntary sector. Hostile take-overs are all but impossible, mergers rare, charities seldom either borrow or lend and domestic charities rarely expand overseas. Many charities might either be bankrupt or have been taken over if they were public companies. The lack of a clear measure of effectiveness means that charities all too often judge themselves, or are judged, by what they can measure which–is income.

Over the past decade the growing focus on income and fundraising has been simultaneously liberating and divisive. Fundraising has helped feed the hungry, find treatments for cancer, house the homeless, save the environment, liberate the disabled, educate children and a whole host of other achievements. Fundraisers can be proud of what they have done.

But fundraising is only a means to an end. Yet the size of charities has become synonymous with effectiveness. Charities have inadvertently taken the commercial model and applied it to their world. For large charities, the Charities Aid Foundation league tables have become a symbol of virility. If a charity hits the top 50 it's in the big time. But if it slips a place in the top ten the fundraising director looks worried and the trustees ask questions. If you ask charities what makes a good year, too many will point to income and expenditure. But there is no clear relationship between size and effectiveness. Some of the largest charities achieve very little and some of the smallest have influence way beyond their size. Fundraising has diverted attention away from the real issue, which is how effective are charities?

These issues have dramatically increased in importance over the past ten years because competition in the voluntary sector is much greater. While charities don't compete in the same way as companies do, they do compete. They compete for money, for volunteers, for staff, for media attention, for a minister's ear, for causes and now for legitimacy.

Up until now charities' response to competition has been to grow or try and get more media attention or batten down the hatches and hope for a return to the halcyon days when money grew on trees, government grants flowed freely and legacies grew year on year.

But charities can respond to competition in a different way. They can change their services and communications to increase the impact of what they do. They can become planters of seeds, rather than millers of corn. This report looks at what charities can do to become more effective and produce the most benefit for the least money. The basic premise is that charities must answer the fundamental question: 'what are we here for?'. Only once that question has been answered clearly can a second question 'what can we do best?' be answered. By answering these questions the organisation will be clearer about its role, and begin to understand what being more effective really means.

2. What is your purpose?

'Cheshire Puss,' she [Alice] began .... 'would you please tell me which way I ought to go from here?' 'That depends on where you want to get to,' said the cat – Lewis Carroll

One of the peculiar aspects of voluntary sector culture is a belief that being a charity is an end in itself. This attitude results in too many charities that are unclear about their role in the world because they grandly believe that what they are doing must be 'worthwhile' because it is charitable.

While few charities do actual harm many could increase their effectiveness by re-evaluating what they are, what their purpose is and what services they should provide. The issue is not only whether an organisation is doing a good job, but how it could do a better one. In a world where the need for the work of charities is increasing, no charity can afford to be complacent.

Charities are often reluctant to talk about being 'better' than other charities. A common argument is that if two charities both have the same objectives and are trying to do similar things it is wrong to even think about trying to be better than the other organisation.

But if you follow this argument through, the logical conclusion is that all charities doing similar things should merge. It is not sustainable to wish to be no better than others but still to want a separate existence. The only justifications for existing as a separate entity are to provide services that are better or different from others or to have a communications or fundraising strategy that positions the organisation differently from its competitors.

Although commercial sector ideas are partly to blame for some charities' lack of clear vision, they also offer ideas for new ways of thinking. Back in 1960 an article by American business professor Theodore Levitt, Marketing Myopia, appeared in Harvard Business Review. He argued that American business was short-sighted because it focused on selling what it had, rather than discovering what its customers wanted. Levitt cited the American railroads at the turn of the century as an example. Because they saw themselves as being in the railroad business, not the transportation business, they nearly went bankrupt. Levitt pointed out that they did not ask the key question 'what business are we in?'.

For companies which don't adapt or don't know what business they are in, competition means that a drop in profits or even bankruptcy looms. Although (bankruptcy) for charities is rare, too many organisations can become moribund, lacking passion, drive and direction. To avoid this every charity must answer the question 'What are we here for?'.

The older the charity, the more important it is that this question is reviewed and clarified. The following examples illustrate that it is a more difficult exercise than at first it seems.

One of the UK's large animal charities was founded 'to care for sick animals' in the early part of this century. Today it runs a series of clinics across the country providing excellent treatment for the pets of those too poor to afford private treatment. Because the founder set it up to care for sick animals, preventative work is still not allowed, resulting in no neutering, no flea sprays, and no worming. It also means that creating a healthy pet population is not in its mandate. It is doomed to always tackle the symptoms, never the causes of those symptoms it treats in its clinics. In response to the question 'what are we here for?' its answer would be 'to care for sick animals' rather than 'to keep animals healthy' and this affects the nature of its services dramatically.

Cancer research charities could be deemed to be here for a variety of reasons: from carrying out cancer research to preventing people dying from cancer or even creating a world free from cancer. This latter vision is far broader than the first, and means that campaigning to reduce smoking and environmental carcinogens and promoting healthy diets all become part of their role.

Yet according to the chairman of one of the big cancer charities its charter forbids it from getting involved in treatment or prevention. However the charter was written at the turn of the century; before antibiotics, gene-splicing and radiotherapy, at a time when the knowledge of medicine was entirely different. Charities should not be restrained by statutes that are even ten years old, let alone a hundred. Their purpose and their work should be based on what is the most effective way of making a difference.

Crisis' former director Mark Scothern (see case studies) recently worked with staff and trustees to redefine Crisis' purpose in relation to homelessness. Its new purpose is broadly 'to bring an end to street homelessness'. Although the organisation is still in the process of assessing the full impact of this change, it has given it an impetus to look afresh at many of its activities.

And while the new mission gives a clear sense of Crisis' direction and the reason for its existence there are a number of ways in which it could be true to its core purpose. It could use its energy to attract more funds from central government for work to end street homelessness; it could focus entirely on using its Open Christmas shelters to contribute to ending street homelessness. Whichever method it uses, Crisis will have to be sure that its efforts are making a clear contribution to the end of street homelessness. Working with people in bed and breakfast accommodation who – whilst not always living in acceptable conditions – may not be at risk of street homelessness, would therefore not be the focus of its work. Crisis' new definition of purpose has brought with it some difficult choices about which services should be provided if it is to be true to its new mission, but it has also brought those choices into stark relief.

Defining a purpose and agreeing on it is not an easy task but there are some key components:

- **Including activities;** A good purpose should include some activities without necessarily defining them

- **Excluding activities;** A good purpose should leave some activities outside the scope of the organisation.

- **Being coherent;** Coherence is subjective, however a purpose should allow you to carry out activities which form a logical whole.

- **Measuring success;** A good purpose will help people understand when they are making progress; success can be measured and understood.

- **Short and simple;** Fifty words (and ideally less than twenty) should be easily enough for a purpose, and everybody should be able to grasp the implications.

An outline of exercises for a trustee/senior management away-day can be found in appendix one. It will help organisations in the process of developing or refreshing their purpose. This may appear to be an idle academic exercise but if a third of an organisation believes its purpose is to run wildlife reserves, a third believes it is to lobby government and a third believes it is to advise land-owners then it will not be surprising if the organisation does not work with maximum efficiency.

It is important that an organisation's purpose should not be seen as a legal definition. While a constitution should be able to weather time without need for amendment and without inhibiting the organisation, a purpose needs to be able to keep pace with changing circumstances and be easily understood. The example of a cancer charity shows how a definition can become legally and culturally restrictive.

Any legal definition should include, at the very least, a catch-all clause which allows the organisation to do the broadest possible range of activities. Barnardo's statute allows it to assist 'children, the sick and the aged'. Macmillan Cancer Relief has a phrase in its memorandum of association which entitles it 'to engage in any activities whatsoever which may lessen the sufferings of cancer patients and as ancillary thereto to protect and preserve the health of their families, friends and helpers'. This kind of clause gives managers the ability to develop new services, which may well have been unimaginable at the time the constitution was drafted.

The ability to refocus an organisation without going through the complicated process of rewriting the constitution is crucial. Charities should be regularly reviewing their purpose – perhaps as often as every five years. This is particularly true for organisations which are growing rapidly or which face considerable external change. The World Wide Fund for Nature took the view that until it had reached a certain size and security of income its purpose was to be a fundraising organisation. Once that size was reached (in the late 1980s) it changed its purpose to being a conservation organisation.

The Campaign for Nuclear Disarmament has struggled to find a new purpose now that the need for nuclear disarmament is perceived to have diminished. And Aids charities have had to adapt their purposes as HIV/Aids and its public perception has developed and changed from a high profile epidemic to a disease which the public has largely forgotten about.

3. Strategies for service provision

It does not matter if the cat is black or white, as long as it catches the mouse – Chinese Proverb

Changing the purpose of a charity is likely to have a profound effect on an organisation's services. The British Red Cross recently redefined its mission which has resulted in a radical streamlining of its services from around 100 to less than a dozen.

The restructuring process is neither quick nor easy, but once an organisation has decided what it is here for, it is then able to decide how it can achieve that purpose most effectively – in other words what services will it provide.

In choosing which services provides charities need to assess which services will have the biggest impact on their beneficiaries and which will give them a comparative advantage or an area of distinctive competence. So after an organisation has decided what it is for, it must decide 'what can we do best?'

It can measure what it does best both in terms of its own skills and expertise and in terms of which services will make the biggest difference to the greatest number of people. This may mean creating services that don't currently exist as well as dropping services that are outside the scope of activities defined by the new purpose or where the impact is less than the new services proposed.

Management writers, Gary Hamel and C K Prahalad have talked about organisations needing to develop their 'core competencies' – the things that an organisation is good at, that mark it out from other competitors and that can be grown and cultivated. This concept can usefully be applied to the voluntary sector.

What are your services?

The first thing an organisation needs to do is agree what its services are. In other words, what is it doing to fulfil its purpose? It is easy to focus on activities which are services in the classic sense, and forget about the rest. Many charities fail to recognise that activities such as membership, PR, lobbying, information-provision, policy, research and awareness advertising are services.

PR is a classic example of an ignored service. It can raise issues, raise profile's, act as a campaign tool, build a brand and so on. For charities where public attitudes matter, it is a key service. For example attitudes of employers and employees are a real barrier to people with disabilities reaching their potential. Disability charities can use PR through both general and specialist media to help change those attitudes. Yet the average charity is unlikely to call PR a service or view it as such.

Defining kinds of services

Charities provide a wide range of services, from running residential homes to lobbying government. Most services fall into four broad areas.

Direct services

Any activity in which a charity works directly with the beneficiary is a direct service. Direct services are what the majority of people think charities do and are what most people give money for. The number of people that benefit from each service is directly proportional to the charity's size.

Advising and influencing others

Charities work with others for a number of different reasons: to make their ideas effective, to reach people they cannot otherwise reach or to empower other groups.

Changing attitudes

There are a variety of ways charities work to change the attitudes of both their beneficiaries and the public. They might want to change beneficiaries' attitudes to their services or to their own lives. Additionally charities might want to educate the public to be concerned about particular issues or inspire people to mount a campaign or to reduce prejudice.

Changing laws and policies

While direct services may tackle the symptoms of a problem, it is often only by changing laws or amending policies that the cause of a problem is tackled. The policies that need changing range from the global to the local and from creating new laws to scrapping or amending existing legislation.

Six strategy portfolios

Below are six strategies that an organisation can adopt for service provision. They can be viewed in two ways. One, an organisation can pick one of the portfolios as a common unifying theme that runs throughout all its services and develop it as a source of competitive advantage. Every service in the portfolio would have the same source of competitive advantage (e.g. being unique). This approach to service strategy is most appropriate for small organisations.

The second model for using the six strategies is to view them as competencies or key skills. In this approach organisations can gain competitive advantage through a combination of core skills. For example its services may both be of a higher quality than other organisations and also have a multiplier effect. Alternatively an organisation could decide that different parts of the organisation will have different competencies. The overseas work may be particularly good at multiplying its impact, while the UK advocacy acts as a catalyst in changing attitudes and legislation.

The six portfolios are set out below:

- **Unique services portfolio:** to do things that nobody else does (either locally or nationally).
- **Beneficiary-based portfolio:** to provide a breadth of services that no other organisation offers to a target group of beneficiaries.
- **Quality or expertise portfolio:** to do things better or differently than others do already, either by having a higher quality of service or a specific area of expertise.
- **A multiplier portfolio:** to have services which are copied so that the impact is multiplied many times over.
- **Social change portfolio:** to be an agent for social change.
- **Profit-making with values portfolio:** to carry out a range of activities which add a clear set of values in addition to making a profit.

1) Unique services portfolio

Two hundred years ago most charities existed to do things that were a matter of life and death because no one else was doing them. Nobody thought about competition, or what the state provided. If the poor didn't have alms or shelter they could die. Without a charitable or church hospital there would be no health care.

Today, life is more complicated. The number of charities that can claim to be doing something that no other organisation (of any size or significance) is doing is small.

The Royal Society for the Prevention of Cruelty to Animals (RSPCA) has a force of over 300 uniformed inspectors in the front line against cruelty to animals. It has an emergency line which takes more than a million calls a year and it is the largest private prosecutor in the UK. While the RSPCA has a range of other services, some of which are also done by other charities, its work is, quite simply, unique.

The Royal National Lifeboat Institution (RNLI) guarantees to reach any mariner in distress within 50 miles of the British Coast. It has a range of craft from inflatables to 65 foot self-righting lifeboats capable of rescues in almost any weather. It estimates that it saves around 1500 lives every year. There is no other organisation remotely like it in the UK.

But more common now are the organisations which had a unique portfolio when they started, but no longer do. For much of the British Red Cross' early life, there was no other organisation able to provide relief during wars or disasters. But during the course of this century the British Red Cross has become more involved in famine relief, and at the same time other organisations such as Save the Children Fund, Oxfam and the UN agencies have started to provides similar services.

The same is true for cancer charities. When it was started in 1902 Imperial Cancer Research Fund was pretty much alone. But now there is a broad range of charities spanning research into different types of cancer and providing treatment, advice and relief. The market place has become more crowded.

Charities need to be aware of the competitive threats they face rather than pretending competitors don't exist. If two organisations are running similar medical research programmes, surely it's better to co-operate and agree respective areas of expertise. If two charities are both serving the same group of beneficiaries, the response to competition can be to improve the quality and breadth of services for those beneficiaries. If charities fail to respond to competition, it can lead to lower quality services, overlap, and perhaps ultimately to the atrophy of one or more organisations.

Organisations whose uniqueness is being, or has already been, eroded, can develop a portfolio in one of the five other approaches that are discussed below.

2) Beneficiary-based portfolio

A number of charities orientate their services, not by offering a specific service or services that are unique, but by creating a range of services to match the needs of a target audience or to further a specific cause.

This approach to services is common in both the medical and social services arena. The Royal National Institute for the Blind (RNIB), British Diabetic Association and many local charities all adopt this kind of portfolio.

The RNIB has more than 60 services. It runs rehabilitation training centres for the newly blind and schools for blind children. It has a braille printing centre, and records books and printed material on tape. It carries out research into the needs of blind and partially sighted people and lobbies parliament and companies to increase the recognition of those with visual impairment. While many other organisations provide services for blind people, none are as comprehensive as the RNIB's.

The British Diabetic Association has a broad range of services for people with diabetes, a medical research grants programme, a bi-monthly magazine for 135,000 members, and an extensive helpline and information service as well as a large branch network. No other organisation comes close to providing this scale and range of services to people with diabetes.

Mind in Camden has a range of over 20 services in the mental health field, all within the London borough of Camden including day care, housing, advice and information, GP advocacy, and legal help.

The beneficiary-based portfolio is as applicable to small local organisations as it is to large national organisations – Mind in Camden's approach to its target audience is a microcosm of RNIB's approach to the country as a whole.

The strength of the beneficiary-based approach is that the needs of the target group are understood and met and services can be constructed without gaps. The danger of the beneficiary-based portfolio is that an organisation becomes a jack of all trades, but a master of none. Each of its specific services may be performed better by another organisation that specialises in that area. As a result charities need to develop a clear response to other organisations providing similar services. They must decide whether to improve their own services, let the services work side by side or withdraw from a particular area of service provision knowing that the audiences needs are now being met by another service provider.

3) Quality or expertise portfolio
The quality or expertise portfolio is based on delivering a better quality of service or a service based on a specific expertise. Either approach can work whether or not there is direct rivalry with other organisations. A charity can decide that part of its purpose is to have services of a higher quality than the alternatives.

The contract culture means that charities are contracted to supply services that the government might otherwise provide. Since the nature of the work is similar whether done by government or charity, the charity needs to be clear that it is delivering better quality services than the local or national government could do. This could mean more people being cared for, or it could mean people getting a higher level of service or even that the effects of the service will last for longer.

Barnardo's (see the case studies) believes that it provides better quality contracted services through a variety of mechanisms which include working with users, cross-fertilising its experience, subsidising services with its voluntary income and working according to its values statement. So far from contract culture being inherently a 'bad thing' because charities are doing the government's work, many organisations view it as an opportunity to improve people's lives. If charities believe in the quality of their work and their expertise, £1m spent with a charity on social services is £1m that should be working harder than it would do in the government's hands.

An organisation can also develop its services to a higher level of expertise than its competitors. To use Hamel and Prahalad's term they have developed 'core competencies' in particular services. For example, WaterAid (see the case studies) is one of a number of charities that aims to provide clean water and sanitation in developing countries. However, it argues that it has developed an expertise or core competence in the creation of water supplies that no other agency has. This competence is based on a range of factors, including working with partner organisations, facilitating government involvement and developing effective models that can be used in different countries.

The Council for the Protection of Rural England (CPRE), which works to protect the countryside, is another organisation that has developed an expertise in working with local and national government. At the local level, it scrutinises every planning application which might have an impact on the countryside. At the national level, CPRE is generally acknowledged by civil servants and ministers to be the environmental organisation that is best at understanding and using the machinery of government to get its message across. It has a core competence in understanding the process of government and is using it to great effect.

4) Multiplier portfolio
Many charities dream of creating a service that takes off like wildfire and impacts on more people than the charity could ever affect directly. While a number of charities have individual services which are multiplied, it is less common to have an entire portfolio of services.

The multiplier effect can work in a number of ways:

• The spread of ideas.
This is probably the most powerful way in which any organisation can have impact beyond those it directly affects. The National Childbirth Trust (NCT) has had enormous impact with its ante-natal classes. Indeed many GP surgeries now run their own ante-natal classes and many NCT classes are run by the participants with no direct contact with the NCT.

• Changing public attitudes.
The Royal Society for the Prevention of Cruelty to Animals (RSPCA) tries to change the public's attitudes towards animal welfare, and Scope aims to change attitudes towards disability and cerebral palsy. More recently, the Snowdrop campaign focused on changing public and political attitudes towards handguns in the wake of the Dunblane tragedy.

• Training the trainers.
An increasing number of organisations, particularly those in the medical arena, run seminars for health professionals who have a direct impact on service provision. The National Asthma Campaign and Macmillan Cancer Relief both run seminars and courses for health professionals to help them improve support for their patients.

Save the Children Fund's (SCF) work with nurseries for mentally retarded children in China (see case studies) is a good example of the multiplier effect in action. The project which was introduced into one region, now covers a population of 60 million people. SCF's intention is to make sure its ideas are taken on in as many regions as possible.

One way for a charity to get its work multiplied is to develop services that are based around ideas, styles of working or methodology. Others are unlikely to copy an idea if they need to spend capital on a building or recruit large numbers of extra staff – though it is still possible. The easiest services to copy are those where there is little or no cost in doing so. The ante-natal classes mentioned above cost GP practices very little to run.

But services don't have to be run for free for a charity to be able to have a multiplier effect. Macmillan Cancer Relief pays for the first three years of each Macmillan nurse's post and after that the NHS Trust takes on the cost of the post. The same is true for Macmillan's medical and social worker posts, although they may also be taken on by academic institutions and social services departments respectively. This means Macmillan's money is acting as a pump-primer. Each postholder aims to increase the awareness of his or her colleagues about the emotional needs of those with cancer.

5) Social change portfolio

Changing society is not an easy task, yet many people believe it is one of the purposes of charities to do so, rather than simply tackling symptoms and ignoring causes. Instead of just opposing what they believe is wrong, charities can also propose alternatives or give solutions. Friends of the Earth (FoE) and Oxfam come closest of the charities in the case studies to being agents for social change.

In order to be an agent for social change a charity needs to have a clear idea of the way in which it believes society is wrong and of how it wishes to change it. There are a number of common threads in this approach:

- **Research is integral to furthering change.**
In order to understand enough to put together a reasoned argument against the status quo, detailed research is crucial. The case study of Oxfam demonstrates that one of the roles of its projects is to help provide evidence for its policy discussions with organisations such as the World Bank.

- **A strong presence in the political arena.**
While many charities have a parliamentary presence this may not be enough to achieve the desired change. Charities can also bring pressure on local authorities and Brussels is important for a number of causes. Oxfam even has an office in Washington to lobby a range of US-based agencies and institutions.

- **Working closely with a range of other organisations.**
Charities may work more effectively with a network of partners. These may be government agencies, individuals, companies or other charities. A network can act in various ways including developing or implementing new approaches as part of the wider picture or working to change the laws and attitudes of government.

Charities that wish to be agents for social change must act as catalysts. They need to spread the effects of their work much further than the actual activities that they can fund and one of the most powerful ways in which a charity can do this is through the spread of ideas. And ideas are cheap to spread in relation to the benefits they may bring. For example, a few years ago Friends of the Earth led the campaign to ban CFCs in aerosols and consumer pressure became one of the main ways by which change was achieved. Once people started making their preferences clear, manufacturers were quick to change the propellant gas they used.

There are similarities between the multiplier and social change portfolios since both aim to multiply the work and ideas of the organisation. The distinctive feature of a multiplier service is that somebody pays for it, even if it is not the originator of the idea, whereas there is usually little or no cost for a service that achieves social change.

6) Profit-making with values
The line between the commercial sector and the voluntary sector is increasingly blurred. Body Shop and Oxfam Trading have many similarities and in the arts world the dividing line is even less clear. The distinctive competence that profit-making charities need is the ability to run a business with the rigour of a company and the values of a charity.

Oxfam Trading supplies goods from a range of overseas and UK suppliers which fit into its fairtrade criteria. It runs a large mail-order operation and supplies Oxfam shops with a range of fairly-traded items. It is run as a company but with the values of the charity.

Able-types is a small charity that provides secretarial, mailing and office services in direct competition with companies. Its workforce is made up of people with disabilities. It is simultaneously providing employment for people with disabilities and running a commercial business and competing on an equal basis.

Integrating strategies for service provision with communication strategies

In the previous *ThirdSector* report *It's competition, but not as we know it*, four strategies for competitive advantage were proposed for the communications and marketing aspects of a non-profit organisation's work.

Niche: Charities can attempt to find a small and defined area of service provision that they can address and own. This niche can be geographical, for example accommodation for the homeless in a particular town. Or it can also be issue-specific, such as the only charity dealing exclusively with a particular medical condition.

Differentiation: Charities which basically do very similar things to other organisations can make themselves different in the public mind by appealing to a different audience (for example a religious audience), by creating a different set of beliefs or way of working or by using a new marketing or fundraising product such as child sponsorship.

Awareness: About a dozen charities try to be competitive by being better known than anyone else. This high level of awareness brings with it benefits such as spontaneous donations and legacies, media interest and credibility in the public mind. But awareness is a risky strategy because the rewards are far lower for second place.

Externally-driven: This strategy works for those organisations which, often due to their history, can survive on the fruits of external events beyond their control.

In the commercial world, generic strategies have been proposed which link all aspects of a company's activities (e.g. cost-leadership). Charities do not work so neatly and there is no single unifying strategic approach to a charity's activities. Instead charities need to have a strategy for service provision and a strategy for (communications) competitive advantage. Having a specific service provision strategy does not dictate that a particular communications strategy is used and vice-versa, though some link-ups are more common. The only link that, by definition, doesn't work is between a differentiation strategy for communication and a unique portfolio for services: there is no need to differentiate services if they are really unique.

4. Analysing your services

Man is a tool-using animal .... without tools he is nothing, with tools he is all
- Thomas Carlyle

The previous sections have talked about purpose, services and core competencies. This section suggests a number of models and analytical tools as ways to review services to identify gaps, duplication, strengths and weaknesses. It should be emphasised that any analytical tool is just that, a tool. If it works well it should provide new insights and ideas. Any tool can be over-used, wrongly used or misinterpreted. Tools are an aid to good management, not a substitute for them.

The Scothern Matrix
This matrix is designed to help managers understand the different status of the services their organisation runs. It can be used to compare services. Columns can be added in or taken out as necessary.

Figure 1. The Scothern Matrix.

Service	Service 1	Service 2	Service 3	Service 4
A. No of beneficiaries				
B. Total Cost				
C. Statutory Income				
D. Fundraising Income				
E. Total service subsidy				
F. Service subsidy per beneficiary				
G. Type of benefit				
H. Profile of service				

[2] *This matrix was inspired by Mark Scothern, though not used by him at Crisis*

The first step in using this matrix is to fill as many of the boxes as possible which will show managers the gaps in their knowledge. Once the matrix is completed key services can be compared by the unit of subsidy per person or the nature of the effect they have on people's lives. The benefit of this kind of analysis is as much comparative as absolute. The matrix allows targets to be set for the level of subsidy or for changing the relative ranking of different services, now and in a year's time.

Notes.

A. Number of beneficiaries
While it may not be easy to measure the numbers of beneficiaries for some services, it is a key ingredient in understanding the impact of a charity's work.

B. Total cost
The additional cost of running any given service or project should be relatively easy to calculate while the fixed cost of staff and overheads is more difficult to assign. But as long as each service is treated the same way it does not matter if the allocation of costs is not perfect.

C. Statutory income
Statutory income is usually defined as coming from national or local government or state-funded bodies.

D. Fundraising income
Income raised from the general public, companies, trusts and the National Lottery specific project is included here.

E. Total service subsidy
This is the gap between the income you receive for running a project and how much it costs in total. This measures how much a service is subsidised from general funds.

F. Service subsidy per beneficiary
Dividing the service subsidy by the number of beneficiaries gives this figure

G. Type of benefit
Note what kind of benefit comes from this service. Examples might

include long-term or short-term, curative or palliative, one-off or recurring, life-saving or life-enhancing.

H. Profile of service

Some services may attract a disproportionate amount of media attention, be vital for fundraising appeals or be the chair's pet project. All these factors can be thrown into the evaluation.

The Wallis grid

Chapters two and three have outlined the types of portfolios of services that charities have. The Wallis grid (figures 2 & 3) enables charities plot their
services against the criteria they have set as being crucial to a project's success. These criteria can also be applied retrospectively to projects that were started before the criteria were introduced. Figure 3 looks at the different kinds of services that were outlined in chapter three and matches them against the actual services provided.

Figure 2: The Wallis grid

Criteria	Service A	Service B	Service C
High profile	✓	✓	✗ (only locally)
Decreasing unit cost (increasing)	✗ (increasing) if anything)	✓	✓ (local authority funding)
Young People	✓ (under 5's)	✓ (over 15's only)	

[3] These grids were inspired by Stewart Wallis at Oxfam, based on ideas that he has used

Figure 3: The Wallis grid

Service Strategy	Unique	Quality or expertise	Beneficiary based	Multi-plier	Social change	Profits with values
Service A	✓					
Service B		✓		✓	✓	✓
Service C			✓	✓		

This analysis can be aggregated up to regional or country level or to departmental level. A further refinement is to combine information from the Wallis grid with that from the Scothern Matrix to enable a gross analysis by type of service against total subsidy and subsidy per beneficiary. By approaching an analysis in this way charities can understand the nature of the services they offer.

The Directional Policy Matrix

This is a standard matrix from the commercial world which allows any two axis to be used and the services plotted. Services can be judged and compared in a whole host of ways:

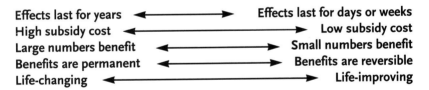

Once the axes are chosen, each service is represented as a circle, with the size dependent on the cost (or the subsidy) of the service. Two sample figures have been created, one showing the number of people benefiting against the length of benefit and the other comparing permanence of results with scale of effect on the individuals. Using the matrix in this way illustrates the different characteristics of a range of services and allows gaps to be identified.

Figure 4: *Directional Policy matrix* – numbers benefiting vs duration of benefit

No. of beneficiaries			
	0-100	100-1000	1000-50,000
Benefit Length			
less than a month	Emergency medical care		Free lunches for the elderly
A month to a year	Psychiatric counselling		
More than a year		Long-term home	Membership and magazine

Figure 5: *Directional Policy matrix* – impact on individuals vs permanence of benefit.

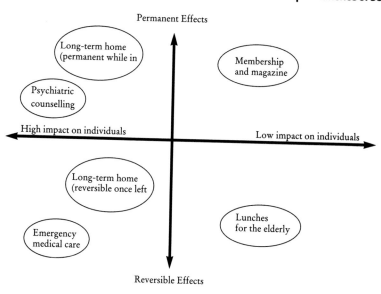

Spectrum of service strategies

Charities need to look at whether their services operate at a number of levels or just in one dimension. The spectrum (or hierarchy) of service strategies presents some ideas about how an organisation can plan its services to be effective in a variety of ways.

Figure 6 shows the core idea of the model and figure 7 shows a worked example for the Royal Society for the Protection of Birds (RSPB).

Figure 6: Spectrum of service strategies

Moral or visionary services
Beliefs or values services
Capability or core skills services
Expertise or product-based services
Local or environmental services

The spectrum of services shows the ways that a charity can try and achieve its objectives through its services. Each of these service strategies represents a different approach to getting results.

Moral or visionary services.

Many charities have a vision of how they would like the world to be. An image of what constitutes right and wrong and the attitudes they would like the public and the politicians to have about the areas that concern them. Some organisations, like Friends of the Earth or Oxfam, communicate that vision strongly and clearly – others are more reluctant to step outside their narrow and sectoral perspective. However, charities can develop a moral leadership role and help set the public agenda as to what are appropriate standards and values for society to hold (see chapter six).

Figure 7: Spectrum of service strategies for RSPB

Moral or visionary services	RSPB believes that the whole environment needs protecting in order to protect birds
Belief or values services	RSPB is actively trying to change the Common Agricultural Policy and change specific agricultural practices
Capability or core skills services	RSPB has core skills in running reserves, research, and membership services to name but a few
Expertise or product-based services	RSPB offers advice to farmers on managing their land
Local or environmental services	RSPB takes specific pieces of land, creates reserves and manages them for environmental benefit

Belief or values services

Many charities have specifics of public policy they would like altered and are prepared to work at influencing the climate of public and parliamentary opinion to change the law or specific departmental policies. These approaches often have specific and usually achievable objectives.

Capability or core skills services

These kind of services are often regarded as 'the real work' – the core way in which an organisation is seen to provide services and do its job.

Expertise or product services

A number of charities have a particular expertise or product as either their core skill or even their raison d'être. WaterAid's expertise is in water supply and sanitation. Guide Dogs for the Blind is in training and supplying dogs to blind people. This kind of service sits along side core skills services in large charities.

Local or environmental services

Many charities have services whose primary importance lies in their location. This means that the service is either designed to supply blanket coverage in a particular borough, is designed to respond to a particular local need or is funded by local residents. The distinction between these and either core skills or expertise skills is that the driving force behind service creation is based on locality, whereas the other two services are created in isolation from their locality. For example, Scope's local partnerships are created by parents concerned to help their own children. Parents in Bromley wants a support group in Bromley. In contrast WaterAid's was founded to have an expertise in water and the specific geographical location of its projects was secondary.

The purpose of looking at services in this kind of spectrum is to identify where an organisation's current services fall, and where the gaps lie. The larger the charity, the more important it is to its effectiveness that it carries out its services through as many of the strategies as it can. By operating at only at one or two levels charities reduce the scale of impact they can make because they are limited only to those they have contact with.

5. Measuring performance and effectiveness

For each non-profit institution, the executive who leads effectively must first answer the question 'how is performance for this institution to be defined?' – Peter Drucker, management consultant

Charities need to know whether they are doing the best job possible with the resources they have. And in any process of organisational development feedback about success is crucial. Yet as discussed earlier, success is much easier to measure in the corporate world where profits mean success and a growth in profits means even more success.

There is no single indicator that makes life so easy for charities. The chief executives interviewed for this report measured success in a variety of ways:

• Monitoring the number of objectives achieved as set out in the strategic plan.
• Measuring the overall income of the charity, particularly when growth in size is both needed and expected.
• The overall awareness of the charity as measured by surveys of public attitudes.
• The level of media coverage.
• The size of the membership, or supporter database, and the rate at which it is growing.
• A gut hunch about the success of individual projects and the effectiveness of the programme overall.
• Simple measurements of programme size, like number of projects or number of people affected.
• The use of performance indicators with varying degrees of sophistication.

Of all the areas discussed with chief executives, it was performance measurement that created the greatest sense of dissatisfaction with the status quo. Only two of the chief executives were able to say confidently that they had performance indicators and even they acknowledged that they were not the whole answer.

Performance indicators

Performance indicators are a simple idea. A set of indices measures or monitors the performance of the organisation in a variety of ways. The finance director in most companies (and in charities) will have a set of indicators which measure financial health. These could include turnover, salary costs, debtor days and outstanding invoices, gearing ratio, liquidity ratios, return on capital and return on sales. Like any set of ratios, they are most useful when compared to the previous month's (or quarter's) performance, rather than viewed in isolation.

The problem for charities is twofold. There is no agreed set of indicators' that can be applied across all charities and it is hard to see how there could be. Secondly, performance indicators are hard work to create and imperfect to use. As a result it seems that most chief executives have put performance indicators to the bottom of their 'to do' list.

The imperfections with performance indicators fall into a number of a broad areas:
• It is difficult to compare like with like with charity services. One service may be residential while another is educational. Some services may change lives permanently while others merely create temporary respite.
• It may take a lot of work to create and maintain the indicators. This may be seen as a distraction from the 'real work' and resented by service providers.
• By creating indicators which are used as a way of managing performance, the work may slowly shift to become more easily measurable and move away from more effective kinds of work which are harder to measure.

But while performance indicators are imperfect and need to be used judiciously, that is not a reason for not using them at all. Directors, chief executives and trustees are there to make the best decisions for their organisations. Without any form of performance indicator they are left to make decisions based on perceptions and gut hunches.

One way to start using performance indicators is to work in those areas which are easiest to measure such as finance and fundraising and get senior stakeholders in the habit of creating and using them. Appendix two contains a list of potential performance indicators to help get the ball rolling.

Process Indicators
Oxfam and Scope have attacked the issue from a different perspective. Instead of using performance indicators they start at the other end of the telescope and have created what could be called a set of process indicators. Oxfam has used its collective wisdom from around the world to create a

set of criteria which it believes will make a project successful and of value to Oxfam. If a project meets the criteria and works within the process laid down, it is much more likely to be successful. This approach empowers Oxfam's regional and country programmes since it allows them to understand the parameters within which they are expected to work.

Scope has taken a similar approach by setting the way that it expects its managers to work (which includes widespread consultation, financial awareness and involved communications) and provided they have acted within that framework, they are empowered to get on with the tasks. This kind of approach does not eliminate the need for performance indicators, but it does try to make sure that services and projects are thought through before they are implemented.

Limitations

Performance and process indicators are a key component of helping an organisation to measure its success, or lack of it. They should never blind an organisation to the need to create a new and more effective set of services.

6. Doing more with less.

Never doubt that a small group of committed citizens can change the world, indeed it is the only thing that ever has – Margaret Mead, social anthropologist

The current world view of charities is essentially that of doers, improving the lives of beneficiaries (directly) by the work they do. But if charities are to have greater impact this view needs to change. The scope of what charities can achieve is severely limited if they must do it all themselves, so they need to move from being doers to being catalysts for change. A number of the organisations discussed have given examples of how they are moving and developing their work. For example, many of the overseas charities realised long ago that they could not do everything themselves – they have been forced to become catalysts in order to become coherent.

This change in approach will bring greater risks for charities. When they are directly providing services they can see the impact on those they work with, even if the numbers are limited. When the goal is to change society the risk of not succeeding is much higher but the rewards are much greater too in terms of the number of people who might be affected. Success for those charities that want to have greater impact will mean taking greater risks, speaking out more readily and even contemplating failure as a part and parcel of normal life. The table below outlines some of the changes in attitude and approach that charities need to make in order to increase their effectiveness:

FROM	TO
The real work is in the services we directly provide	The real work is whatever we do to get us closer to our goal
We can only speak out in areas where we have direct experience	We have a clear set of beliefs. We will speak out based on those beliefs
We are doing the government's dirty work	The government has taken on the funding of our social services work

The government's agenda in this area has been set by a policy think tank	→ The government's agenda in this area has been set by charity 'ABC'
We run 200 classes for teenagers across the UK	→ The idea has spread so rapidly that we have no idea how many classes are happening
The behaviour of companies in this area is terrible	→ Any company breaking our guidelines will be avoided by our ethical investment fund
A spokesman for the CBI said this was a good budget for companies	→ A spokesman for NCVO said this was a good budget for charities
Tony Blair was assiduously courting corporate leaders today	→ Tony Blair was assiduously courting charity leaders today
Charities should keep out of politics and stick to their proper role	→ Over the past twenty years, charities have become more influential and effective
I give my money to help charities do good work	→ I give my money to make sure we see effective change in society

New roles for charities in a changing world

There are three main ways in which charities can have more impact in the competitive times ahead. They can act as moral leaders, act as standard setters and be the creators and spreaders of ideas.

Charities as moral leaders

There are huge areas of public policy where politicians' ideas have been discredited, and the ideas of charities could spread like wildfire. If charities want to see society change, they must provide moral leadership and generate ideas for change. They must speak out when they see things they believe are wrong.

Morality, in this context, can be defined as the behaviours, attitudes and standards which society accepts as right and wrong. Some morals will be the same as our laws (like murder) while others will not (like attitudes to abortion).

Currently charities rarely give moral leadership – or at least it rarely gets into public thinking. In all the recent debates about knives, poor schooling, nursery education and violence on TV, charities' voices have rarely been heard. Yet it is unlikely that children's charities do not have a viewpoint on issues of importance to millions of children.

The issue here is not about specific policy or laws but about charities influencing what society sees as right or wrong. Part of the problem is that political correctness makes charities reluctant to develop spokes people who become familiar faces in the media. A rare example is Friends of the Earth's former director Jonathan Porritt who became a leading spokesman for the green movement as a whole in the 1980s. He became a household name and Friends of the Earth was able to influence people's thinking beyond its size. The charity world needs more media figures if it wants to have more influence.

Moral leadership requires a change in thinking by charities on what they feel able to speak out on. Traditionally charities will speak out on areas in which they believe their experience has given them a specific insight. In order to give moral leadership, they will need to have a strong framework of beliefs which allow them to conclude what is good or bad for their constituency in isolation from their specific experience.

For example, a children's charity may decide that it has no specific experience which gives it a view point on the national curriculum, so in the traditional model it would keep quiet about it. However it may believe that all children need to be 'educated for life' and in the new model of speaking out on it's beliefs it could voice a strong view on whether the national curriculum helps or hinders.

Nobody will ask charities to be moral leaders, just as nobody asked Gandhi, Wilberforce or Martin Luther King to be moral leaders. It was the strength of their ideas and the conviction and power with which they communicated them that made these people moral leaders. Charities too can be moral leaders. The opportunity is there for those who wish to take it.

Charities as standard setters

Charities can take moral leadership one step further and set standards which are better than existing laws or government policies, and to which people or organisations will voluntarily adhere.

In many areas of public life there is a growing call for a definition of what good behaviour looks like. For example, in the environmental field there is much criticism of the terms 'environmentally-friendly' and 'recyclable'(sic) because they are vague and unspecific. So any company that believes these adjectives describe it or its products are left without many choices. They could set their own standards, but that would lack credibility. Alternatively they could stop using the terms – but all their competitors would continue to do so. So they continue using them despite the weaknesses.

However, were the company wanting to describe its products as 'cruelty-free' or 'animal-welfare friendly' or 'organic' it would be very difficult to use these terms in an unspecific way. The Royal Society for the Prevention of Cruelty to Animals (RSPCA) has set up a separate charity called Freedom Food to implement its farm animal welfare standards (see box) and the Soil Association has long had an accreditation scheme for those farmers and retailers who wish to call their product organic.

It isn't just in the environmental arena that standards are unclear. With the introduction of the Disability Discrimination Act there are a host of employers who need to understand what discrimination looks like and how to change the standards they set in the workplace. In education, schools want to know whether they are producing well-rounded children. In the NHS, hospitals want to know whether they are looking after patients adequately. While the government has introduced its citizens' charters these don't always cover all the areas of concern and the government is likely to be seen as a flawed supplier of standards.

Some of the overseas charities have formed a consortium to produce and market Cafe Direct fairly traded coffee. Up till recently the decision to produce their own product, rather than agree a standard, limited the amount of equitably-produced coffee on the market and did not encourage existing coffee producers to change their methods. But following the launch of the FairTrade Foundation standards have been agreed for a range of products.

A parallel campaign has been launched by overseas charities to produce standards for clothing retailers. The tension for standard setters is between commercial-reality and genuine improvements in conditions. If standards if can be met with minor changes by the bulk of existing producers they are easy to introduce but risk being pointless. Equally there is little point in producing standards that can only ever be met by a very limited number of suppliers since little real impact will be achieved. It would be foolish to see standards as simply working through the physical production of materials. Ethical investment is also a powerful way of setting standards by forcing companies as a whole to meet particular standards. A number of charities have dabbled in ethical investment, particularly to make sure their own reserves meet certain standards or at least exclude certain unacceptable companies. However the number that have used ethical investment as a tool for rewarding the behaviour of companies that set high standards is limited.

The success of those who wish to set standards is dependent on the power of the consumer. It is because consumers want to buy products that reach certain standards that companies are prepared to meet those standards. If the consumer, the employee, the parent or the patient, is not interested in the standard, or not prepared to pay a necessary premium, then the standard will not flourish. However setting standards remains an extremely effective of making an impact many times greater than that an organisation could achieve working directly.

Freedom Food

Freedom Food was set up by the RSPCA in 1993 to improve welfare standards for farm animals. For many years, the RSPCA had campaigned to change the law on factory farming. Freedom Food approached the issue from the consumer and commercial angle. By setting standards across a range of species such as laying hens, pigs, turkeys, sheep and beef, it has encouraged farmers and retailers to improve conditions for animals, knowing that their effort and investment should improve the salability of their produce and bring approval by the world's largest animal welfare organisation.

Freedom Food is self-funding through levy and royalty payments from

---

both farmer and retailer. Any farmer or supplier who wishes to be accredited to Freedom Food has to be visited by an assessor, and demonstrate compliance with the scheme's standards. Members are monitored by specialist RSPCA staff and any supplier found breaking the standards is expelled from the scheme. From public launch in 1994 the scheme has mushroomed to include 2000 stockists, including Tesco, Safeway and the Co-op. It is estimated that 15% of laying hens are now reared to Freedom Food standards, and by the end of 1996 approximately ten million animals had passed through the scheme at an approximate cost of 10p an animal.

More importantly, new investment in farm animal production is increasingly expected to meet Freedom Food standards, even for those outside the scheme. One major retailer has told all its suppliers to phase out sow tethering in the near future, and the country's largest pig abattoir has spent millions of pounds changing its procedures to meet Freedom Food standards.

Freedom Food is not perfect and a tension remains between animal welfare and commercial practicalities. It will be well into the next decade before the majority of meat is produced to Freedom Food standards, but for an investment of under £1m, the RSPCA has changed the nature of commercial animal production in a way that legislative change never could.

Charities as spreaders of ideas

A good idea can be taken and used without cost to the originator. In the commercial world this can mean that good marketing ideas are plagiarised as soon as they are in the public domain. In the voluntary and public sectors, the use of other people's good ideas is inherent in the culture. The spread of services through ideas can be extremely effective. In the medical arena, the spread of ideas is faster and more efficient than in many other areas. Charities like the National Asthma Campaign and Macmillan Cancer Relief try to give health professionals new ideas about how to treat their respective illnesses. In the overseas arena, Oxfam and Save the Children Fund view the cross-fertilisation of ideas between countries and continents, as one of their most important and effective ways of working. In less than 30 years social norms have changed. Prospective parents go to ante-natal classes and fathers are an integral part of the birth plan, cancer care is seen as an integral part of cancer treatment and patients are allowed to die with dignity in hospices or even their own home and protection of the environment has become part of public consciousness.

Charities can change ideas in a variety of ways and with differing timescales:

Education and attitudes
A number of charities have education programmes in schools and for the public. The timescales for the impact of these changes can be as long as 25 years, but once attitudes have changed they are deeply ingrained in people's consciousness.

Policy changes.
Government policy is often deeply influenced by the thinking of specific individuals or think-tanks. These ideas can often create a policy shift and lead the government agenda in a dramatic fashion. For example Mrs Thatcher's adoption of environmental issues was alleged to be a result of Sir Crispin Tickell's intervention. While charities rarely lead the government's thinking they have done so in specific areas such as third world debt relief, and the opportunity exists for much greater influence.

Both these areas represent important shifts in the way that charities do business. The charity is no longer confined in its impact to what it can directly do itself. Its work, its influence, its impact is multiplied many times. An imaginary example of this new style of charity is outlined in the box.

Parents for Life – The perspective from 2017
Parenting is the most difficult task that anyone will ever undertake. Just as each set of skills is learnt, new ones are needed. Yet society gives little or no support to parents. It's far easier to learn about the nine months of pregnancy than the decades of parenthood that follow. Moreover the parental difficulties of childcare, nurseries, schools, exams, teenage sex, and careers have no champion in the public arena.

It was for this reason that Parents for Life was set up in 1997. In the past twenty years, Parents for Life has successfully made lessons and self-help groups for parents the norm, rather than the exception. The groups span the range of children's ages helping parents to discuss and share their

---

experiences as their offspring grow, and some have little formal contact with the main charity.

Parents for Life has a flourishing membership of 500,000 people with many parents recruited at its ante-natal classes or soon after the birth of their first child. Its magazine is carefully adapted to suit the needs of its members as their children grow. Off the back of the membership there is a thriving mail-order business.

The organisation has succeeded in making employers more friendly towards parents through its parent-friendly accreditation scheme which sets down standards for employers to meet on paternity leave, crèche facilities, flexitime and other issues. Public places have not escaped as accreditation can also be awarded to parent-friendly public places that provide baby changing rooms, small toilets and play areas.

Parents for Life has also changed attitudes towards parents and parenting. People have realised that disruptive children are often the results of poor parenting and that both parents need to be involved from an early age in the child's development.
Parents for Life has been set up in 14 countries as a result of the British model. While the exact nature of the organisation varies from culture to culture, the basic fact remains that people in all societies have welcomed the chance to be better parents.

Conclusion

Charities face a simple choice as they plan for the coming decades. They can decide to do nothing to increase their effectiveness, thereby marginalising their impact on those they exist to help. Alternatively, charities can strengthen their efforts to make every pound go further than ever before.

At the most fundamental level this means charities must be clear about their purpose. They must know the answer to the question 'what are we here for?' Importantly they must be clear what makes their services special and have a strategy behind their service provision. This report has suggested six strategies for increasing the impact of services. Not only does every charity need to be clear which of these strategies it is following, but it needs to be able to measure the impact of it services and see that impact increase.

So at one level the answer to the question 'what are charities for?' is a simple one. Each charity must answer the question for itself and in doing so maximise the impact it has on the world. This alone would give rise to a stronger, fitter voluntary sector.

But charities have the potential to do far more than just a better job. They exist because of what they believe in. The roots of most charities are in visions of a better world. Yet those visions, those beliefs, those values are all too often hidden. The beliefs are there, but the passion has gone the fire in the belly, the outrage and the anger long extinguished by layers of hierarchy, working parties and procedure.

If charities rekindle their passion, they could give society a new set of beliefs, new inspiration and new ideas about the values and ideals of the world in which we live. They could place themselves as moral leaders and the source of new and innovative ideas to tackle some of society's intractable problems. Charities have a unique place in our social fabric. The experience of providing direct services gives charities an untarnished and objective insight into the world as it is. They could use it to create a climate which makes lasting change possible.

Part 2. Charity Case Studies

The case studies that follow are based on interviews with the chief executives (and in two cases members of senior staff) of each charity. The interviews were designed to understand how each organisation approaches service provision and bridges the gap between what its mandate allows it to do and its financial or human resources. Supplementary material was drawn from annual reports and internal documents.

Barnardo's – Roger Singleton

Barnardo's is one of Britain's largest children's charities. It runs more than 250 projects and helps 30,000 children every year. The types of project that it runs fall into five main areas (the figures in brackets indicate the percentage of total childcare expenditure):

• Families with young children (16%)
• Children and young people with disabilities (27%)
• Children needing families (13%)
• Disadvantaged young people (20%)
• Children and young people with educational need (21%)
• A further 2% is spent on research

In addition Barnardo's spends considerable sums on informing the public and other childcare professionals about its work.

Roger Singleton describes the 'funnelling' process by which Barnardo's decides how best to help children. The organisation's memorandum and articles of association are the starting point. They allow provision of services for children, the sick and the aged. The second part of the funnelling process is to apply the filter of a set of criteria called 'in greatest need'. These look at a number of descriptive approaches to the need for service provision. Two of the filters are to see what access to resources are already available, and what funding would be needed from voluntary income.

The dilemmas facing Barnardo's are acute. Its own figures suggest that one child in four grows up in poverty, yet clearly it can only help a fraction of these children. Moreover it is not always possible to help those in greatest need.

Barnardo's direct service provision is overlaid by a drive to disseminate information about 'what works' in childcare through lobbying and public education. In contrast to the relatively small number of children that are helped by the childcare projects on which between 90 and 95 per cent of expenditure goes, the information and lobbying might help many millions of children, but the chances of success are much lower. Singleton makes it clear that Barnardo's credibility to inform and lobby is firmly rooted in the power of its direct experience.

Since much of Barnardo's funding comes from local government, it is important to know whether there is something that makes a project distinctively 'Barnardo's'. This is clearly a much more difficult question. Barnardo's distinctiveness lies in its approach and process, not in the actual projects that it runs. This means the added value from Barnardo's is much more subtle and intangible.

It is also difficult for Barnardo's to measure success, let alone value for money. As Singleton points out 'When is a child successfully adopted – when a family is found? After a year? After ten years? It's equally difficult to judge the impact of a project for disabled children. How much is it worth to give a disabled child a more normal life?' At the moment Barnardo's bases these judgements on its years of experience of childcare work.

Barnardo's is a classic provider of charitable social services. Its income is approximately half statutory and half voluntary. Although it is moving more towards 'campaigning', the vast majority of its time, energy and expenditure is geared to direct service provision. Its primary strategic approach to service provision is to take money from government and spend it more effectively.

Crisis – Mark Scothern

Crisis started in 1967 when a group of people got together to raise awareness of street homelessness in East London. They raised funds for the handful of homelessness projects that existed in Central London and a couple of years later they opened Christmas Shelters for the homeless – Crisis at Christmas was born.

In 1990 when Scothern took over, the charity was an effective fundraising outfit. It was interested in expanding its activity and considered focusing on one of its key activities – fundraising, grant giving, campaigning and direct services. It had raised £2.4m and had a complement of six full time staff supported by a host of volunteers and some temporary staff.

Crisis now has over 30 full time staff and many temporary staff help over the winter period. It runs five programmes:

• **Christmas and winter services.** The biggest project is the London Open Christmas service and Crisis also supports smaller Opens and temporary winter services around the country. These are the focal point of the bulk of Crisis' fundraising and communications work, but much less so than they used to be.

• **Emergency Accommodation.** This is focused on Crisis' Open House programme which aims to develop the temporary winter services into all year round projects providing direct access for homeless people from the streets to permanent housing.

• **Mental health outreach services.** Based on work Crisis supported in Manchester, this programme aims to offer expertise and funding learned from other parts of the country. Crisis is keen to work with statutory agencies to commission mental health outreach services.

• **Resettlement into private rented sector accommodation.** The core of this programme is formed by rent guarantee schemes. Crisis is experimenting with offering a rent guarantee scheme franchise aimed at local authorities.

• **Basics.** Crisis has set up Fareshare in central London which re-distributes surplus excess fresh food from supermarkets and other suppliers. Also included in this programme is the provision of clothing to homeless people on the streets of central London.

In the busy, competitive world of housing and homelessness agencies the difficulty for Crisis is knowing exactly what its role is and what its key strengths are. Three years ago, Scothern initiated a strategic planning exercise which resulted in Crisis re-defining its ultimate goal as the 'end of street homelessness'. This new purpose forced Crisis to look at its services afresh and continues to provide the charity with major management challenges. It is considering which areas it should concentrate on, what the effect of bolstering some services at the expense of others would be, which services help it to achieve its ultimate goal most effectively and how will the work fit in with the programmes of other agencies.

Since 1990 the government has committed over £200 million to the Rough Sleepers Initiative. This programme has reduced the number of street homeless people in central London from approximately 2000 to 300 at the latest count. Of all the organisations spoken to in this report Crisis seems closest to its ultimate goal, partly because of efforts to quantify the problem.

This reduction in numbers has brought new pressures for the organisation. It must ensure that its work does not stop prematurely and it has to take into account the maintenance work that will have to take place to prevent people coming onto the streets in the first place.

Crisis started life as a volunteer-led organisation and a conscious decision was made to bring in professional staff. As a result of changes in street homelessness and the growth of Crisis in size and complexity, Scothern believes that trustees will have to get more involved again. Not only will they need to define more clearly the beliefs and values of the organisation, but also to provide greater support to the organisation's senior staff.

Crisis has been a highly effective fundraising charity and is searching hard to increase the effectiveness and contribution of its direct services. The challenge now, as the prospect of ending street homelessness seems more likely than ever before, is to maintain the pressure and develop the skills base to adapt the organisation's activities to a rapidly changing environment.

Friends of the Earth – Charles Secrett

Friends of the Earth has a simple goal – to create an environmentally sustainable society where we are in balance with resources and with nature. The sheer scale of this task means that it is not possible for FoE to directly do everything that is needed to transform society.

Its role has to be one of catalyst, of multiplier and of collaborator. At the same time the organisation has to tackle of some of the more direct environmental issues, such as habitat loss or inappropriate road schemes. At one level, this gives Friends of the Earth what Secrett sees as an almost spiritual role, and certainly what he would call moral leadership in persuading society to reassess what it believes and how it behaves. Foe believes in 'democratic', not coercive, change so the power of reason is paramount. Unlike many charities, FoE sees itself as having a clear role in the spread of ideas about environmental protection and sustainable development. It can be most effective by being a kind of environmental think-tank, about sustainable development in particular.

Underpinning Friends of the Earth's approach to campaigning and change are a set of values. It believes that well researched and argued cases are a powerful force for change and that if people or governments know the reality of a situation they will often change their minds. Its second core belief is that it must tackle a greater breadth of activities than traditional environmental issues such as democracy and constitutional issues, economics and Europe. Thirdly it feels that a critical mass of people need to become environmentally active in a whole range of roles, from shareholder to voter, if change is to occur. It also believes that it cannot simply oppose destruction, but also must also propose solutions. FoE has five campaign teams: transport and air pollution, energy and climate change, biodiversity and habitats, industry and pollution and food and biotechnology. While direct campaigning still has a major role in FoE's work, Secrett now aims to knit individual environmental campaigns into the much larger economic, social and political fabric of life. Measuring progress towards a sustainable society is not easy. There are a variety of methods that Secrett uses to judge the organisation's effectiveness. One is the extent to which FoE's ideas have become accepted wisdom. Another is the tangible success of a variety of campaigns. For example imports of mahogany have decreased by 80 per cent since FoE launched its campaign.

It is Friends of the Earth's role as a catalyst and agenda setter that not only makes it an interesting contrast to other non-profit-making organisations. Its role is to make the wheels of change turn, but not necessarily to turn them itself.

Macmillan Cancer Relief – Nicholas Young

Macmillan Cancer Relief is much more than Macmillan nurses, though they are the dominant feature of its service provision. It splits its services into four main threads. Firstly direct service provision in the form of over 1500 nurses and 150 Macmillan doctors, secondly £5m in patient support grants, thirdly a building programme of about £8m a year providing improved facilities for people with cancer and lastly an education support and information provision programme.

Young is keen to point out that Macmillan also invests heavily in public understanding about cancer care, through its advertising, fundraising and extensive range of literature.

Nonetheless it is Macmillan's relationship with the National Health Service that makes it most interesting. Every nurse is initially funded for three years by the charity and after that is funded indefinitely by the local NHS trust. Despite the constraints on NHS funding no trust has broken its agreement with Macmillan. In effect Macmillan is unlocking NHS funds by using the seed money of the first three years' funding. Macmillan nurses help to increase the understanding of other health professionals, who may only meet two or three people with a specific type of cancer every year.

There is a strong policy dimension to Macmillan's work. Not only has it managed to shift NHS thinking and expenditure at trust level, but the Chief Medical Officer has recently announced a rethink in the organisation of cancer care, to which Macmillan contributed and which it is now a key plank of Macmillan's strategy to support.

Macmillan calculates that it helps between 200,000 and 300,000 people out of a possible one million people living with cancer in the UK. Its postholders span the spectrum of cancer provision from hospital to community.

Since every Macmillan post is co-funded the creation of new posts is far more complex than looking for gaps in the geographical service, and is a delicate balance between local needs (as assessed by the regional directors) and the willingness and ability of the local NHS trust to take up the funding after the Macmillan pump priming period. In addition the first three years of funding for each nurse needs to come from a local Macmillan nurse appeal. The poorer the area the harder it is to raise the money. Lottery and corporate funds are being developed in order to allow greater ability to work in areas of high need.

Macmillan also funds four small associated cancer care charities. This approach to service provision allows the beneficiaries of the British Colostomy Association or Breast Cancer Care independence and a much greater sense of ownership, while still having income security.

Performance measures in relation to service provision are difficult for Macmillan, because the charity does not employ the Macmillan nurses and doctors – they mostly work within the NHS. However the charity does work with them to help satisfy the NHS's demand for outcome measures and evaluated performance.

National Asthma Campaign – Melinda Letts

The National Asthma Campaign was formed in 1989 as the product of the merger of three smaller asthma charities. It is the dominant asthma charity in the UK. This determines, to a certain extent, the services it must provide, since it aims to 'conquer asthma through a combination of research, education and support'.

Its need to provide a range of services creates an 'ongoing tension' as to where to put resources. Resolving this tension is at the heart of the strategic planning process, and the subject of many debates between senior staff and trustees. Research is the largest single form of expenditure with approximately £2.5m budgeted in 1997. This research expenditure includes a number of permanent research posts and an active grants programme, administered by a research committee.

Because of the priority given to the research programme, education and support programmes are under constant cost pressure. National Asthma Campaign runs a helpline, staffed by asthma nurses, for those with asthma, which attracts far more calls than can get through, due to a limited number of lines. Finding the funds to extend the helpline has formed a major part of the budget tension in the past year. The support from the helpline is supplemented by information booklets and other materials, a network of branches and information-based membership.

One of the parts of National Asthma Campaign's work of which Letts is most proud is its work with the NHS and government. It has just been 'contracted to manage NHS research and development into asthma management'. NAC is the first charity to be awarded this kind of contract. Letts has worked hard at developing the relationship with government and the NHS because by itself NAC could only help a small fraction of the people who are likely to use the NHS's asthma services.

The National Asthma Campaign does not use formal performance monitoring, but it does use a comprehensive set of objectives, monitoring and appraisals, backed up by what Letts describes as gut feeling. The strategic planning process is strong and senior managers need to be able to justify their ideas in front of their peers. In order to strengthen the development of strategy, a clear demarcation has been made between operational issues and strategic issues. The former are chaired by Letts' deputy and the latter by Letts. This is part of a wider process to empower people in their day to day working and change the culture in the organisation in order to increase its flexibility and innovation. For National Asthma Campaign and Letts, the development of the right culture and the right processes are an integral part of the need to deliver an ever improving portfolio of services.

Oxfam – David Bryer and Stewart Wallis

Oxfam has a very broad mandate in its articles of association: 'to relieve poverty, distress or suffering in any part of the world'. This mandate is refined every five years into a statement of 'strategic intent' which in Bryer's words answers the question 'what are we best fitted to do?'. From this five-year framework, a series of one-year and three-year plans are developed which deal with practical operational issues.

Oxfam has programmes in over 70 countries around the world. In each of these countries it has a three-stranded programme of development, relief and advocacy. It is this three-cornered approach replicated in each of its programmes that Oxfam believes marks it out from other agencies. Not only is every country part of the whole, but it aims to replicate the whole. In addition, Oxfam uses its experience on the ground to feed up into a wider perspective. It is these linkages that Bryer and Wallis believe make Oxfam's work especially powerful. Even if a programme is effective on the ground, it must also feed into the wider programme. Key questions in understanding the value of a project are 'what can others learn from this project?' and 'how does it help our advocacy work?'.

The relief work is only partly an exception to this model. Oxfam would always respond to urgent and desperate need, but it would also want to work to find long-term solutions.

Oxfam is always working to improve the impact of its work. Wallis has been reviewing what he sees as Oxfam's comparative advantages over other agencies which he cites as:

• Local knowledge

• Capacity building of partner organisations

• Each programme combines development, relief and advocacy

• Emergency response expertise and capacity

• Scale of international activities and ability to influence key governments and global agencies

It is none of these factors alone that give Oxfam its edge, but a combination of them working together. As a result of identifying its comparative advantages, Oxfam has been changing its programme. It is working with less partner organisations, but working harder to strengthen them. It is reducing the number of its overseas offices, but increasing the remaining offices' involvement in resource allocation.

With a programme as complex as Oxfam's, measuring impact is not easy. The projects are easiest to study – beneficiaries can be interviewed, heads counted for each unit of money or resource. But measuring the impact of advocacy and the value of linkages is often more difficult. For example how much credit should Oxfam take for changing a specific policy of the World Bank? Bryer and the other directors are concerned that the organisation's priorities could be distorted by the relative ease of measuring some activities compared with others.

To overcome these problems Wallis and Bryer have introduced a set of criteria which act as a sieving process to ensure that any projects that come up for approval have been thought through. The criteria range from 'ability to have an impact' to 'strategic importance to Oxfam'. The decisive factor is often a gut hunch from those involved.

Royal National Institute for the Blind – Ian Bruce

RNIB is the largest supplier of services to blind and partially-sighted people. It currently has over 60 services operating from more than 40 sites, reaching about 150,000 people. It aims to double this number over the next five years.

RNIB is user-led and needs-led. It has 103 trustees, the majority of whom have some kind of visual impairment. They represent the spectrum of people using RNIB's services and organisations of, and for, blind and partially-sighted people. The trustees make up 45 committees on all of the aspects of RNIB's services and work. By having such a comprehensive representation RNIB is able to speak for both the users of its services and the wider blind community.

RNIB also has a strong research department which has carried out a number of pioneering pieces of work to establish the needs and situation of blind people. In 1991, it discovered the extent to which the majority of blind people live in poverty and that although elderly people were those most likely to be visually impaired they were disproportionately low users of services.

As part of a five year plan, RNIB has identified four priorities:

• Challenging blindness – raising awareness and tackling discrimination

• Extending services to more blind and partially sighted people

• Increasing the priority it gives to older blind and partially sighted people

• Improving the quality of services to users and supporters

These priorities are underpinned by a constant review of individual services to assess their impact. This means that within the overall portfolio of services a number are introduced, and some may be withdrawn or scaled down over any given period. Geographical coverage, length of time over which people may benefit, amount of subsidy needed and alternative service suppliers are all criteria by which these judgements are made.

Bruce points out that it is very hard to compare the value of different services. He gives the example of education, which may benefit somebody for another 50 years, but carries a high subsidy. In contrast, the talking books service improves the quality of life in old age (the average user listens for 12 hours a week) and for many is a psychological lifeline and carries a relatively low subsidy. It does not however stop an elderly blind person being either alone or poor and only benefits a person on average for seven years. Which service is better? Which deserves a higher priority?

Bruce has introduced strong performance measurement data (over 1000 measurements) within a performance and marketing framework and covering the range of services. He has developed something called 'a unit of service subsidy' in order to increase the comparability of different services. He points out that measuring the quality of services is much more difficult than measuring the quantity.

Royal Society for the Protection of Birds – Barbara Young

The RSPB is Europe's largest wildlife conservation charity. Its income has doubled in the last five years and its breadth of activities has also increased. It is no longer simply a 'bird conservation' organisation, even though that remains the public perception. It is also the major funder of Birdlife International, which takes action for bird conservation around the world.

Young has developed the organisation to be what has been called the ultimate example of 'entryism'. In other words it starts where people are at, with an interest in birds, but develops their interests into habitats, biodiversity and even environmental economics. RSPB describes five areas of its work:

• Leading research on birds, conservation and the environment

• Campaigning to protect wildlife and habitats

• Managing places for nature

• Providing advice on land-use and wildlife issues

• Informing and educating through its adult and children's membership

These areas are interconnected and give RSPB a range of ways to operate. At one extreme it can buy an area of land to help a specific endangered bird population. At the other end of the spectrum it can campaign against specific agricultural or economic policies that have a major effect on birds and wildlife across the UK. In between these two extremes are a whole range of ways of operating, such as putting evidence together to oppose planning applications, in which the RSPB acts in the interests of birds and the environment.

The strength of the RSPB lies in its ability to have a broad range of services, so that changing laws or policies, or hearts and minds is not a bolt on extra but an integral part of its work. At the same time, it has all the appearances of a traditional 'reserve-based' conservation organisation.

The way that the organisation does its business is clearly an issue for Young. The approach to strategy is divided into 'ends objectives' (saving or conserving birds or habitats) and 'means objectives' (changing detrimental policies or influencing key audiences). This approach means that while income is important, there is a measurability about what the organisation hopes to achieve which allows success to be evaluated in a whole breadth of ways.

On top of the strategy process, every member of staff and key volunteers are being trained in the core communications values of the organisation, so that they are clear what messages RSPB wants to get across to its publics. This consistency of approach will help to make the society more focused and influential in its conservation work, as well as hitting its target of a million members in the near future.

Save the Children Fund – Mike Aaronson

Save the Children has set itself an enormous task. It exists to create a better world for children, by acting as an agent for social change on their behalf. Unlike most development agencies it has not limited itself to developing countries or to the UK. It runs projects both here in the UK (though these are being scaled down), and across the third world.

The sheer size of the task means that SCF has moved in recent years from the simple direct service provision such as immunisation and primary health care to being a catalyst for helping other agencies. It is working both at the micro-level in individual countries and the macro-level with national bodies such as the Overseas Development Administration and international bodies such as the World Bank. The breadth of SCF's experience gives it both a clear idea of what works and the ability to translate that experience into a variety of settings.

Aaronson denies that SCF is only scratching the surface with an example of how a single project can have a massive impact. An integrated education kindergarten project for mildly mentally retarded children was started by SCF with one social worker in a province of China. Other local authorities have adopted the idea and by the end of 1997 there will be 100 kindergartens covering a population of 60 million people. Other provinces are now interested and the concept may one day cover the whole of China.

In the UK, SCF is providing mainly end-user service running crèches and family centres. Recent budget cuts have meant that SCF has decided to withdraw from, and where possible hand over, many of its existing UK projects. The irony is that SCF and other overseas agencies have known for years that they can't do everything for themselves in third world countries and have developed services accordingly. In the UK, Aaronson believes that the dilemma has not appeared so stark and so social service providers have not been forced to develop services with an built-in multiplier effect.

The strategic planning process at SCF is a constant search for how to do more with less. SCF has always attempted to develop innovative solutions to child-related problems and then pass that knowledge over to other players. Aaronson cites the example of a more effective approach to re-uniting children with their families in disaster situations which SCF has pioneered and is now in the process of empowering other agencies to use. In the UK, SCF is trying to change people's attitudes to children and childhood, on issues like children's access to health and education services, and their participation in decisions that affect their lives.

SCF does not have any formal kind of performance indicators which can be used across the board. It judges effectiveness on a qualitative basis through the professional skills of those involved. Since SCF covers such a broad range of skills, it has not been able to develop specialist indicators for particular areas of work.

Aaronson has been forced to make tough choices recently, as SCF has seen its income shrink after the boom in the 1980s. This has presented the organisation with problems but it has rammed home the message that SCF must 'work smarter, not harder' if it is to achieve its goals. For Aaronson, a leaner, fitter organisation, with a clearer, more focused vision will be better equipped to tackle the problems ahead.

Scope – Richard Brewster

Scope (formerly the Spastics Society) is the leading charity providing services to people with cerebral palsy and related disabilities. Its aim is for people with cerebral palsy to gain full human or civil rights and have the full resources for their needs.

It has been through significant changes in the past few years. In 1994 the organisation changed its name in order to shed the old image of 'spastics' and took on a wider mandate in relation to disability. Scope has just agreed to introduce individual membership with the ability to vote trustees onto the governing body. This will give individuals the opportunity to feel that the organisation more directly represents them and to become a trustee.

At the same time, the organisation has been restructuring in order to clarify the relationship between service provision and funding, in particular those services which are state-funded and those which are not. Scope's council has asked for better financial health, including an annual surplus and healthy and growing reserves. The restructuring has created two operational divisions, one for contract services and one for local partnerships and community development, funded by voluntary donations.

Scope provides services in a variety of ways. It offers residential care and support, it helps young people with conductive education, it works in partnership with a variety of groups to help them provide local services, it campaigns on both political issues and public attitudes as well as working to give people better employment rights.

In the 1950s most people with even mild cerebral palsy would be in institutions, while today many are able to live in sheltered housing and are wage-earners. Scope's dilemma now is deciding what it's role should be. The role of service provider is now more about influencing mainstream education than running schools or more about changing the attitudes of employers than being an employer.

Change in a user-led charity like Scope cannot possibly be decided by the chief executive alone. Brewster and chair Anthony Hewson have been at the heart of Scope's changes in equal measure. Their job has been to discuss and consult with a wide range of users, staff, and other stakeholders. Change, in Brewster's view, must be participative if it is to succeed. So while he views his and Hewson's job as to lead, it is not necessarily to decide. The corollary of this is that the process and the style through which management needs to work to be effective is clearly determined by directors with decisions being pushed down the organisation. This style is a cascade of empowerment, in which people are aware of the parameters (financial implications, quality of service, impact on fundraising or marketing, the need for widespread consultation, strategic context etc.) but are able to make their own decisions.

This style means that the organisation needs to have a tight control on performance measurement. It has made some attempts at measuring the impact of its work and one of Brewster's tasks on becoming chief executive was to review the organisation from top to bottom. The result is that a new formal performance measurement process is due to be introduced in 1998.

Tommy's Campaign – Helen Otton

Tommy's Campaign exists 'to give babies the best possible start in life' by researching into premature birth and foetal health. It is the youngest charity (started in 1992) in these case studies and has different tensions to cope with. The development of service provision has been in two areas. The creation of a grants programme for medical research into illnesses during pregnancy and premature births. The driving force behind the creation of the Tommy's Campaign is the grim fact that the rate of premature births has not changed since the second world war, despite the medical advances made in so many other areas of human health.

Grant applications are reviewed by two external referees before being scrutinised by a research committee. It has set out clear guidelines for applicants and through a funnelling process tries to ensure it gets the highest quality applications. There is a limit to how many applications will match all the criteria from existing research programmes so Tommy's campaign is in a process of deciding which areas it believes need greater medical attention and will now aims to set up research programmes possibly through permanent funding of clinical research posts.

Otton has given Tommy's Campaign clarity by focusing on its mission, vision and corporate strategy. This has eased discussion about the relevance of a range of suggested areas of work. For several years, Tommy's Campaign has organised the Parent Friendly Awards, getting people to vote on which companies and services were the most 'parent-friendly'. The difficulty is that this bore little relation to Tommy's mission, vision or corporate strategy, but was a good corporate fundraiser and publicity vehicle. In the future it will have a diminished role. New initiatives such as a 'National Pregnancy Week' which match the corporate strategy of 'raising awareness of... the issues surrounding prematurity' and 'communicating ... about the ways to reduce the risk of a complicated pregnancy' will take precedence.

The dilemma is still focused on which services to provide. Otton has been actively lobbied to start a 24-hour pregnancy advice line, and a network of support groups. While these services are within the strategic framework, they need a greater level of human expertise and resources than Otton believes Tommy's would prudently be able to commit to.

The link between services, financial demands and strategy is one which Otton weighs up clearly.

Although Tommy's Campaign is a young organisation, effectiveness still needs to be assessed. In the research programme, the number of papers in journals, the completion of research projects and ultimately the practical application of research projects, are all measures of success. Raising awareness and spreading information are measured by levels of media attention or requests for information. At a cruder level, three years ago the Campaign was only funding research in St Thomas's hospital and is now funding over 20 projects nation-wide.

WaterAid – Jon Lane and Stephen Turner

WaterAid has a clarity of purpose, even a passion, which pervades the whole organisation. It is to give people access to clean water and sanitation in developing countries. That clarity of purpose is vital, since the task is enormous compared to its size (income is between £7m and £8m a year) and age (it started in the early 1980s).

The organisation's style has had to evolve as it has developed and grown. In the early days it provided grants on a one-off basis, but now it has long-term relations with partner organisations. It has also changed the actual work that is done, from predominantly an engineering-led programme of well-building, pipe-laying and hole-digging to a facilitation role. Within each country, and with each partner organisation, the WaterAid approach is to redirect or reorganise local resources 'to give people access to clean water and sanitation in developing countries'. The country programmes are now empowering others to do the tasks they used to do themselves. WaterAid remains clear about what it won't do which includes water for agriculture, Eastern Europe, emergency water supplies and countries where it can't work with partner organisations.

Its approach within an area can take a number of forms. It may be to work with a partner to provide low-cost water and sanitation, which then acts as a template which other organisations or local governments can follow. It may be to help local organisations to work together to provide water. It may be to show that enormous dams or capital outlay aren't needed. The model also effectively caps the amount of work WaterAid will do in an area. An expansion of the programme means to cover more geographical areas, not to provide water supplies directly. This empowerment approach also applies to helping organisations get funding from other institutions and helping 'partner organisations to develop their capacity to undertake integrated water projects' as its strategy suggests.

WaterAid's recent strategic planning identified advocacy as one of its key objectives. This is a clear recognition by WaterAid that by influencing multinational bodies such as the World Bank, the IMF and the Overseas Development Administration, it can potentially do far more than it can achieve through its fieldwork. Lane and Turner also want to influence individuals and are looking at input into relevant postgraduate courses in development studies or civil engineering.

Its ability to evaluate success is mixed. The WaterAid approach suggests that country partners might become independent and indeed this has happened in Zimbabwe. WaterAid estimates that it has provided clean water to three million people, but finds it hard to measure performance on a country basis other than by qualitative judgements. Lane and Turner still see considerable growth potential for WaterAid, and plenty of work still to be done. Growth will result in 'more countries and more areas within countries'.

Part 3. Acknowledgements

Inevitably a huge number of people is responsible for the stimulus to create ideas in a report such as this. The biggest thanks go to the people who gave up their time to be interviewed; Mike Aaronson, David Bryer, Richard Brewster, Ian Bruce, Jon Lane, Melinda Letts, Helen Otton, Mark Scothern, Charles Secrett, Roger Singleton, Stephen Turner, Stewart Wallis, Barbara Young, and Nick Young. I would also like to thank my clients, Barnardo's, Friends of the Earth, Leonard Cheshire Foundation and National Asthma Campaign whose business has, without them realising it, let me have the time to do this project. Phil Bembridge had sufficient faith to agree to publish this report well before it was written. Julie, Daniel and Megan have been great in putting up with my writing.

About the author

Joe Saxton is director of campaigns and national services at the Royal National Institute for Deaf People (RNID) responsible for PR, policy and research, lobbying, campaigning, information services and typetalk.

For five years he worked at direct marketing agency Brann Ltd, latterly as deputy client services director covering a range of charity and commercial clients. Before Brann, he worked in Oxfam's appeals dept.

He has talked and written extensively on marketing issues in the voluntary sector, covering branding, direct marketing and integrated communications. He was the principal author of the *ThirdSector* report *It's competition, but not as we know it.*

He is a trustee of the Royal Society for the Prevention of Cruelty to Animals and chairs its international committee. He sits on Friends of the Earth's finance committee.

Your response

Hopefully the ideas in this report have stimulated readers and given them insights into their organisations. They are not the definitive word on any of the issues covered, but are aimed to help readers to develop their own ideas and to stimulate discussion. The report has been left unreferenced in order to make it a smoother read, but details of any publications referred to are available from the author. Readers can contact him on phone/fax: (01865) 865767 or email: joesaxton@aol.com.

Comments for publication in *ThirdSector* are welcome. Please send them to Gerard Dugdill, Editor, *ThirdSector*, 4 Assam Street, London E1 7QS Tel: (0171) 247 0066 Fax: (0171) 247 6868 email: thirdsector@api.co.uk.

Appendices

Appendix 1. A day to think about who you are.

These are a number of exercises and suggestions for an away-day for senior managers or trustees.

Exercise 1. Name those services.

Divide into groups of four. Brainstorm what services your organisation offers. Estimate how many people each service helps and the cost per person. Compare each group's conclusions.

Exercise 2. Agree a common purpose

Create nine pieces of paper the size of playing cards. On each of these put a simple definition of what your charity's purpose might be (e.g. to do cancer research, stop people dying from cancer, do lung and stomach cancer research and so on). Arrange people into groups of three or four and ask them to prioritise the nine definitions in the shape of a diamond.

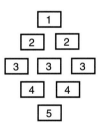

The card at the top of the diamond is the one that the group feels most powerfully describes your purpose over the coming few years. The next layer is those definitions that next best describe your purpose and so on. In the process of this exercise much discussion will hopefully have taken place about the best purpose for the organisation. Once each group has agreed its diamond, feed back into the group as a whole and try to agree between the whole group. It may well be that a new definition of purpose arises.

Exercise 3. How would you like your charity to be different in five years time.

Every person has to write down three ways that they would like the organisation to be different in five years, with one top choice. The long wish list is compiled with asterisks by the top choices. The group can then try to agree its common priorities and create a long list of five or ten changes.

The same exercise can be repeated with achievements and measurements of success. These three choices of priorities are subtly but importantly different. For example the organisation might decide in the first exercise to set up a campaigns and parliamentary unit, its achievement would be to get new legislation passed and its measurement of success would be to halve the number of people in care.

Exercise 4. What are your core competencies?

Using the same technique as in exercise 2, create nine cards with different services, or different competencies on them and prioritise them into a diamond according to which services or competencies give you a comparative advantage over other organisations working in the same area.

These exercises are only suggestions and any of them can be adapted freely. In addition, participants may decide to have some more formal presentations on individual services.

Appendix 2. Potential performance indicators

This list of performance indicators is neither definitive nor comprehensive nor even necessarily relevant for every organisation. It is intended to stimulate managers into thinking about what is relevant and achievable for their organisations.

FINANCE AND FUNDRAISING

- Months of expenditure available on current level of reserves
- Percentage of total expenditure derived from different income sources (e.g. legacies, statutory, covenants, etc.)
- Salaries bill as a percentage of total expenditure
- Fundraising costs as a percentage of total expenditure
- Income assured beyond this financial year (e.g. grants, bankers orders, investments, etc.)
- Number of new donors/committed givers per year on a moving average, number of lapsed donors (not given in 24 months) and net size of database
- Number of total legacy pledgers and number and size of legacies.

ADMINISTRATION

- Number of staff in administration as a percentage of those in service provision
- Number of staff in IT as a percentage of those in service provision
- Number of fundraisers as a percentage of staff in service provision
- Turnover of staff per year

SERVICES

- Number of beneficiaries overall and for each service
- Number of staff per beneficiary by service and overall
- Cost per beneficiary overall and for each of the main areas of service
- Number of information requests on a rolling average
- Number of press mentions on a rolling average
- Number of contacts with MPs on a rolling average
- Capital cost of buildings per beneficiary and per unit

Help your organisation deal with new challenges facing the sector...
..by buying more copies of
.*What Are Charities For?*

Simply complete the details below and send or fax back to *ThirdSector*

YES I would like .... extra copies at £2.95 each (for *ThirdSector* subscribers)
I would like .... copies at £4.95 each (for non-subscribers)

Title................................... Name...................................

Job Title...

ThirdSector Subscriber no...

Address...

....

Postcode .... Tel...................................

Fax .... Email ....

☐ I enclose a cheque for £....... made payable to Arts Publishing
International Ltd

☐ I wish to pay by Mastercard/Visa/AmericanExpress/DinersClub
and authorise you to debit my card for £.......

Card number ☐☐☐☐☐☐☐☐☐☐☐☐☐☐☐☐   Expiry date ☐☐☐☐

Billing Address (if different from above) ....

....

.... Postcode ....

If paying by credit card this form can be faxed back to *ThirdSector*
fax no. 0171 247 6868 If sending a cheque, enclose this form in an envelope
(no stamp needed) and address to: *ThirdSector* Subscriptions Department,
Arts Publishing International Ltd, FREEPOST LON 6577, London E1 7BR.